SKETCH

Like an Architect

SKETCH
Like an Architect

Step-by-Step From Lines To Perspective

DAVID DRAZIL, MSc.

Thank You!

Dear sketcher,

Thank you very much for purchasing this book. I believe it will bring you a couple of 'aha-moments', valuable and practical information, inpiration as well as tools for practicing and becoming better at sketching.

I'm beyond grateful for your support of the #SketchLikeAnArchitect project.

Happy Sketching!

David Drazil, MSc.
www.SketchLikeAnArchitect.com

Contents

Is Hand Sketching Dead?

In today's era of virtual and augmented reality, hyper-realistic visualizations, and 5D BIM technologies, is there still a demand for hand-drawn sketches and illustrations? With universities, students, and professionals being focused more than ever on new technologies, parametric design tools, or robotic manufacturing - why is it still beneficial to be able to sketch?

COMMUNICATION

First of all, it is about communication - about being effective in communicating your ideas. It's not about you talking and other people hearing what you say - it's about making sure that these people understand exactly what you mean.

If you can sketch your idea with a pen and paper, you can convey it with any other visual media. Knowledge and skills gained through hand--sketching help you become better even as a digital artist.

Observation skills, confident lines, understanding of perspective and light and shadows - all of that will help you make better architectural visualisations, conceptual diagrams, digital paintings or any other illustrations.

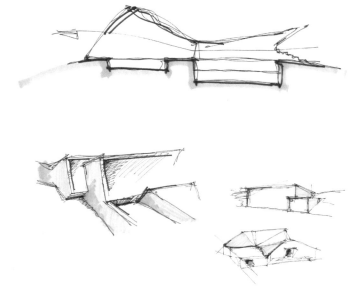

Sketch To Understand Things and to
Make Others Understand You

Is Hand Sketching Dead?

STATE OF FLOW

Already when I was yet a student in architecture school, I heard from my professors all the time that students didn't sketch anymore. Instead of sketching out solutions or drawing different options of elevations, students just rather jumped right into their BIM software to place default windows into generic walls and were done with the facade. Such process, where you dive into software without being clear on what you want to achieve, hurts both you as a designer and the design itself. There is a missing piece in that process – the part where you can clarify your decisions with an advantage of instant connection between your head and your hand. The part where you easily get into the state of flow and have your creativity at its peak. Even when you're a super-user of a digital software, the connection doesn't happen that smoothly because of the technological barrier between what you imagine in your head and the output from that software.

WHY SKETCHING?

From my point of view, there is a demand – even a growing demand – for hand-sketches that clearly communicate ideas. With the ability to sketch, you can quickly, easily, and naturally present and communicate your ideas. However, it's not only about presenting the final result. Sketching serves extremely well even (or especially) during the process.

By sketching you can brainstorm new ideas, solve problems, shape your design and make iterations to optimize it. A free-hand sketch, with all its imperfections, often opens a dialogue, invites viewers to participate in the process and suggests with welcoming arms that nothing's set in stone.

Good free-hand sketching connects us on a very human level. Even in today's world focused on innovative technology, I find hand-sketching with pen and paper absolutely irreplaceable.

Reading Guide

The main body of this book consists of 6 Steps. Each of these Steps is divided into 4 parts (as seen below). First, I explain you what we are going to learn and why. Then, I show you the techniques and I give you some crucial tips & tricks. After that, you can learn by practicing on the provided worksheets. Finally, there is an exercise for each of the Steps, so you can apply and test your newly acquired skill or technique.

I believe in learning by doing. And I also believe that learning needs to get a bit hard in order to work. Please, don't just read this book - use the worksheets in this book for practicing new skills and techniques. Only then you'll get the most out of it - and that's the point. Please enjoy!

What & Why

What we are going to learn and why this skill or technique is important for architectural sketching.

01

Tips & Tricks

Techniques and advice on what to do and what to avoid. It is more of a guideline since any rule can be broken.

02

Learning

Practice makes perfect! It is applicable for sketching, too. You can use the prepared worksheets to help you start.

03

Applying

Time for a final exercise, where you can apply newly acquired skills and the techniques you have practiced.

04

Lines & 2D Objects

If you look at most architectural sketches, they are made of a number of different lines. Some of them are wavy, jagged, zig-zag, and some are straight. They are used not only for contours, but also for guidelines, constructional lines, shading, hatching and texturing – pretty much almost everything in a drawing!

As the first step, we're going to learn to draw different types of lines. We start with relaxing our hand, getting familiar with the right posture and correct movement of our arm, and drawing various types of lines.

Different types of lines

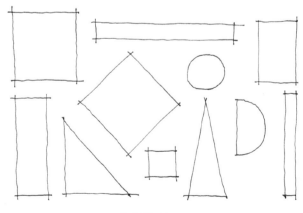

Basic 2D objects

Line Types

Wavy

Staggered

Zig-Zag

Jagged

Dotted

Dotdash

Solid

WORKSHEET 01.a

Wavy

Your turn!

Staggered

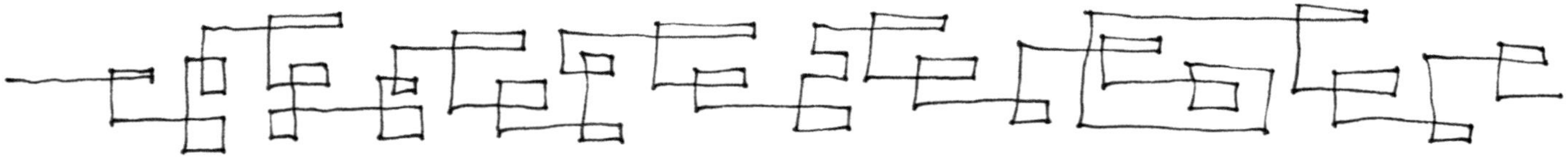

Your turn!

Zig-Zag

Your turn!

Jagged

Your turn!

Dotted

Your turn!

Dotdash

Your turn!

Solid

Your turn!

Drawing Straight Lines

For the construction of 2D objects and perspective views later on, we will need to practice sketching straight lines.

The best technique for practicing straight lines is to connect two points with the shortest possible line.

Basically, we are going to need 3 types of straight lines according to their direction - **horizontal, vertical, and diagonal.** All of them will be very useful in the later stages of our architectural sketching.

Practice drawing straight lines in different directions with the **Worksheet 01.c and 01.d** on the next pages. When drawing straight lines to the center point, it's important not to rotate the page and to get comfortable with various directions of your strokes.

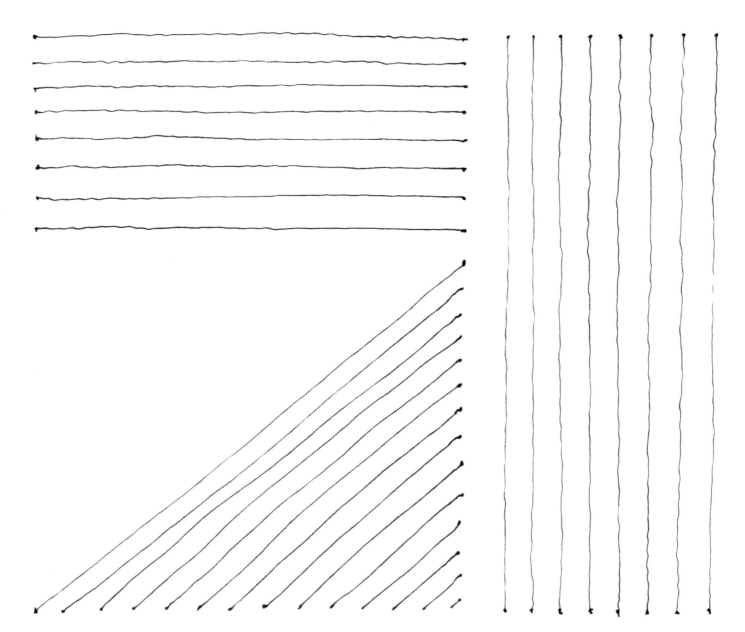

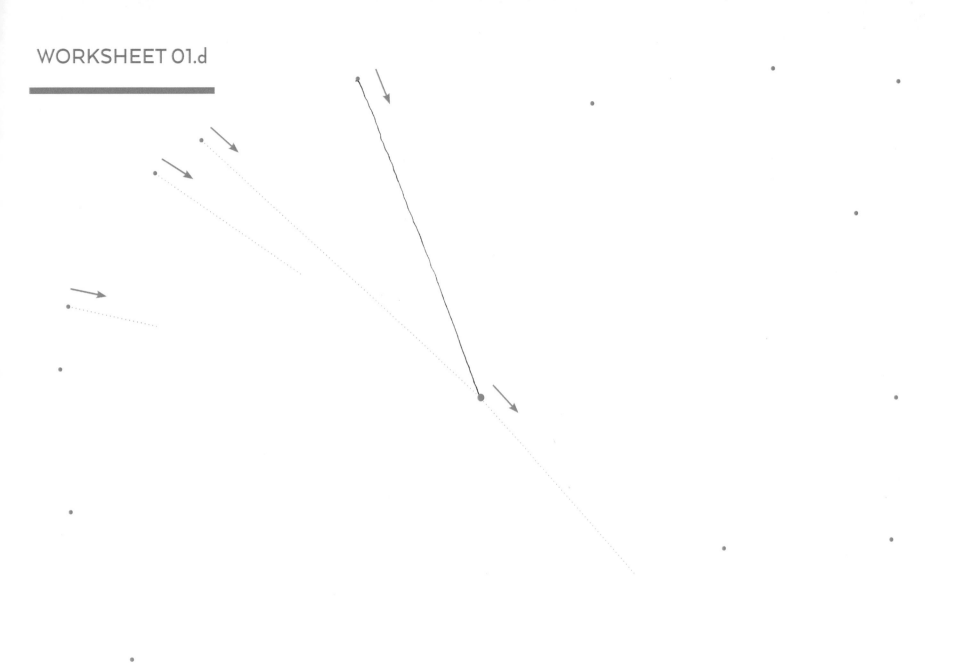

Drawing 2D Objects

Once you become confident about drawing lines, you can move on to drawing some basic 2D objects. Typically, what we are going to need further on in the process are squares, rectangles, triangles, and circles or semicircles.

When drawing 2D objects, **it is important to draw each side of an object with a single stroke**, as shown in the explanation below.. It is not recommended to overdraw a line with more strokes as it only gets a bit messy ;) Try to draw only one line even if it's not perfect. Just practice more of them, they'll get better.

Another great tip is to **always connect two lines of an object without leaving a gap in between**, even quite the opposite - **create intersections** in corners. It will add a bit more technical look to your sketches.

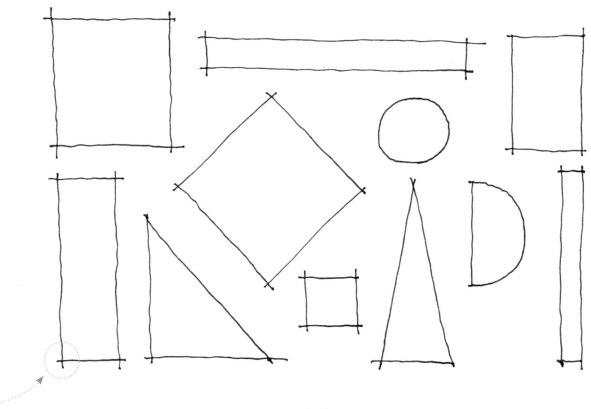

Basic 2D Objects

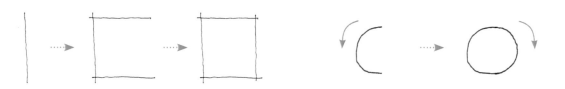

The process of sketching 2D objects

WORKSHEET 01.e

Exercise

Your Exercise for practicing Lines & 2D Objects is to **sketch a simple cityscape of your favourite city**. If you cannot think of any city, feel free to get inspired by your own photos, search on Google, Pinterest, or any other platform of your choice.

The point of this Exercise is not to get too complex, but to still practice different types of lines, long straight lines, various 2D objects, and also to get familiar with the use of lineweight.

Don't worry too much about making it look perfect, the focus should be on becoming more confident about the mentioned techniques when drawing lines and 2D objects. Good luck!

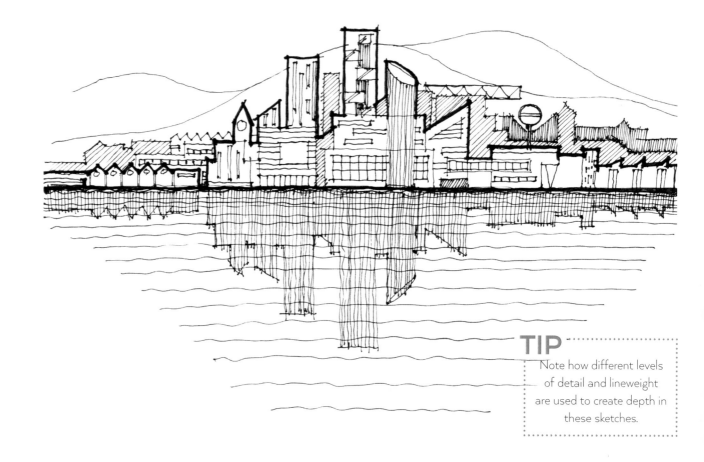

TIP

Note how different levels of detail and lineweight are used to create depth in these sketches.

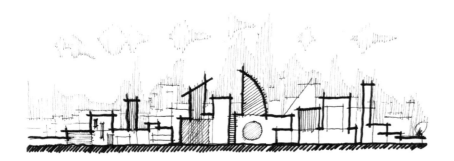

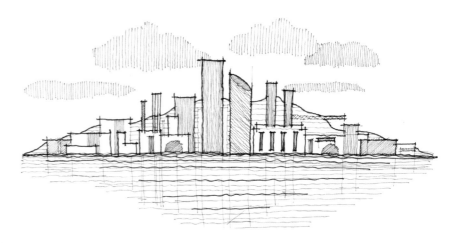

Wrap up

Let's sum this up! On this page you can find the most important tips & tricks for sketching Lines & 2D Objects. These advice should serve as guidelines, but feel free to use what suits you the best and leave the rest out with no worries.

#01
Mind your posture and maintain a good overview of your canvas.

#02
Draw with whole your arm, starting the movement from your shoulder.

#03
Always draw with a light hand; pull your pencil/pen rather than push it.

#04
Do not erase the incorrect lines – learn from them instead.

#05
Use of different lineweights serves well for defining depth planes, better clarity, and creating emphasis and contrast in a drawing.

#06
Long lines are achieved by drawing with your whole arm and supporting your hand by sliding on your little finger.

#07
2D Objects – draw each line with a single separate stroke.

#08
2D Objects – create intersections in corners, avoid leaving gaps.

Step 02

Basic Perspective Rules

The way we see the world is driven by rules of perspective - both linear and atmospheric. In this chapter we'll take a look at one point and two point linear perspective as it will lay the foundation for our architectural sketches.

The important thing about perspective is to realize that it is applied everywhere, literally everywhere. Everything we draw, from an apple to a spaceship, needs to follow the rules of perspective in order to look realistic.

> Perspective works like an invisible grid helping to place objects in our spatial composition. It is a way how to describe 3-dimensional space on a 2D plane.

There is no reason to be scared of perspective drawing, it doesn't always require a ruler or math knowledge to handle it. By following just a couple of simple rules, you'll be able to express your spatial ideas through sketching in perspective. Let's dive into it!

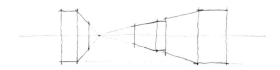

1-point perspective

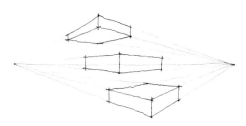

2-point perspective

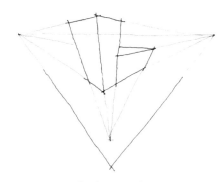

3-point perspective

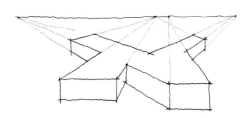

Multi-point perspective

Concepts of Perspective

Let's have a look at the diagrammatic sketch on the right hand side of this page. Simple sketch of 1-point linear perspective illustrates its main components which we will further refer to. See the description in the tip-box to fully understand the key elements of every perspective.

TIP

The key components of any perspective drawing are Picture Plane, Horizon Line, Vanishing Point, and Ground Line.

Picture Plane is an imaginary transparent plane the 3D space is projected onto.

Horizon Line is an imaginary horizontal line at eye level.

Vanishing Point is a point on the horizon line, where parallel lines appear as converging.

Ground Line is parallel to the picture plane and the ground.

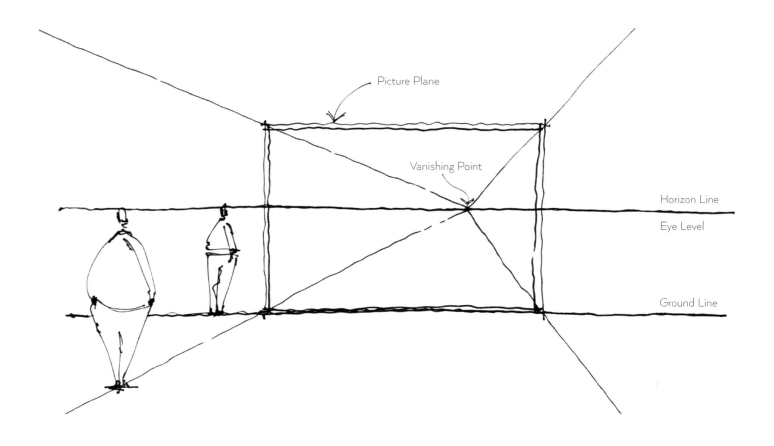

Picture Plane

Vanishing Point

Horizon Line

Eye Level

Ground Line

More on Perspective

On the illustrations on this page you can explore the rules of perspective through a comparison of a Top View and a Perspective View of the same scene. Notice the position of the observer in the Top Views and how it is translated into the Perspective Views.

These parallel lines in the Top View converge at the same Vanishing Point (VP) in 1-Point Perspective.

The parallel lines of this direction converge at the Vanishing Point 1 (VP1) in 2-Point Perspective.

The parallel lines of this direction converge at the Vanishing Point 2 (VP2) in 2-Point Perspective.

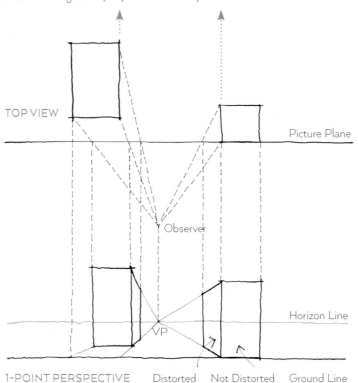

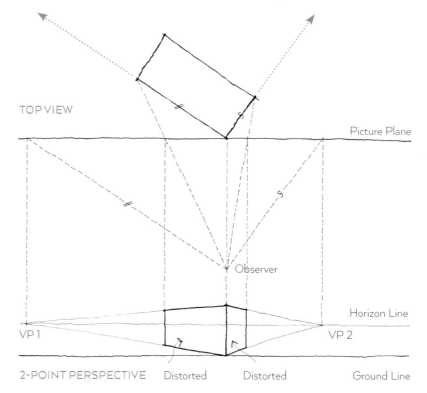

View in Perspective

Time for a quick demonstration! Take a box or any box-shaped object close to you and place it on a table in front of you. Because the box is now positioned under your Horizon Line, you are able to see its top surface. If you raise the object above your head (above your horizon), you will be able to see its bottom surface. Well, this is not rocket science, I know, but it dramatically helps to understand the importance of the position of a Horizon Line in relation to displayed objects in perspective. See the different positions of the Horizon Line on the right hand side of this page.

Find Worksheets 02.a-d on the next pages which will guide you while practicing free-hand perspective sketching.

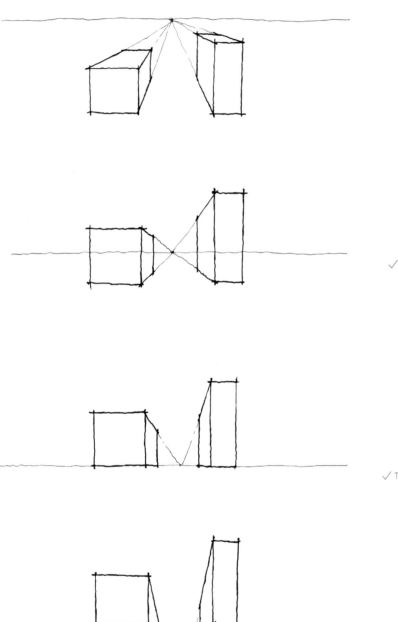

✓ The Horizon is above the Objects. We can see the top surfaces.

✓ The Horizon is cutting through the Objects. We can't see either top or bottom surfaces.

✓ The Horizon is aligned with the Ground Line. We can't see either top or bottom surfaces.

✓ The Horizon is below the Objects. We can see the bottom surfaces.

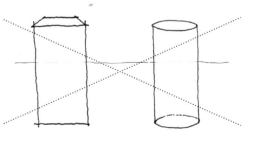

✗ Horizon is cutting through the Objects. We shouldn't be able to see the top surfaces!

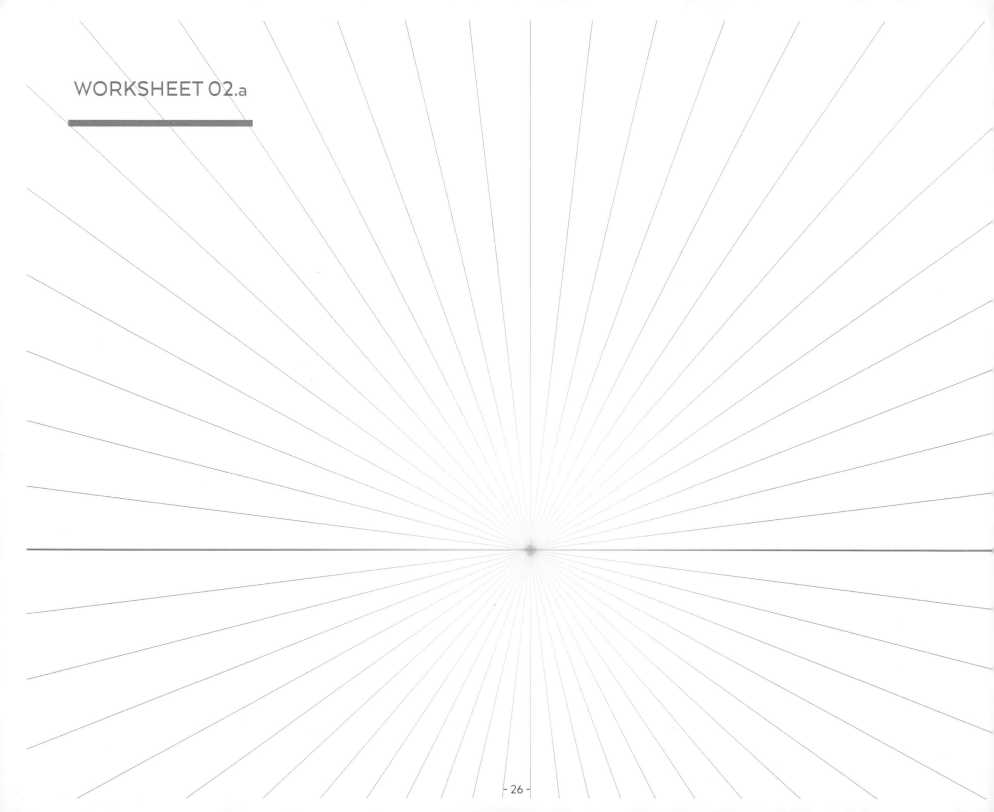

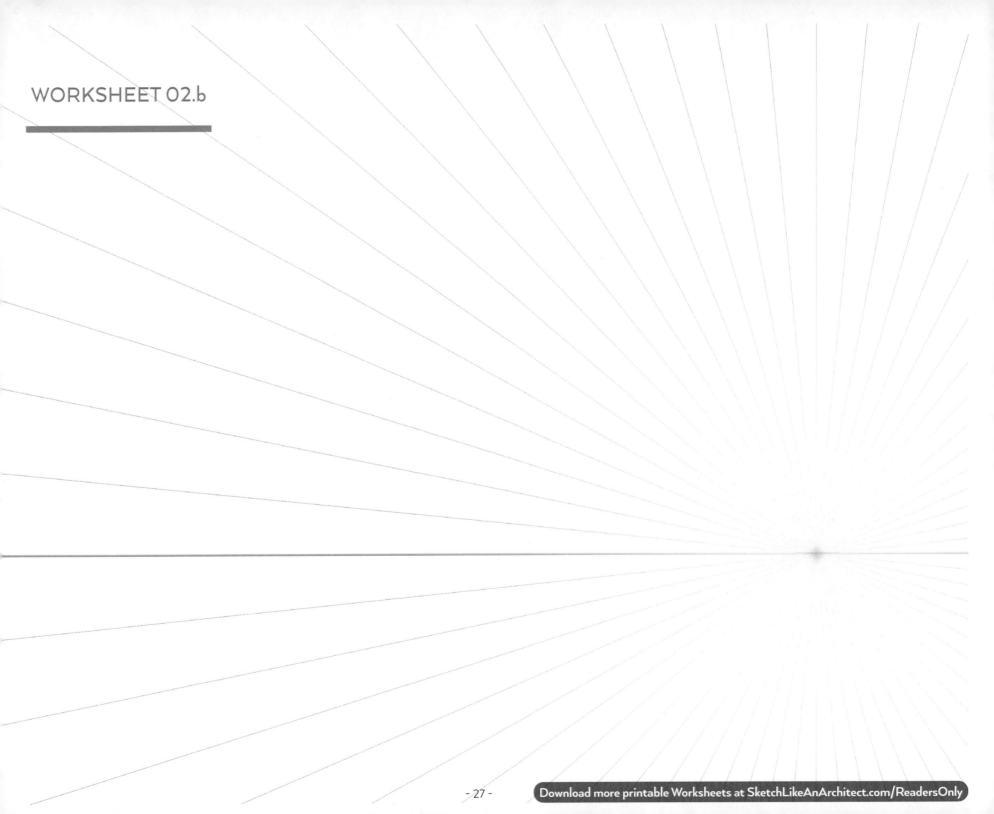

WORKSHEET 02.b

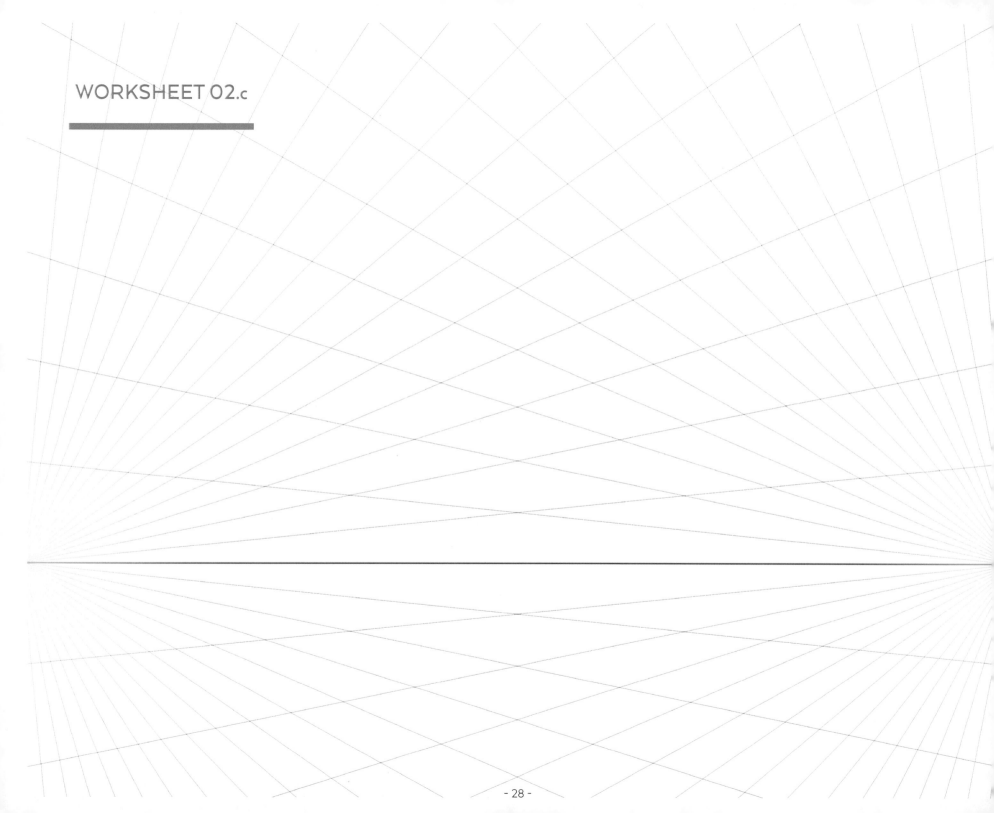

Exercise

Your Exercise for practicing Perspective is to **create a free-hand (1-point or 2-point) perspective sketch displaying at least three volumes of your choice.**

First, I recommend to start with placing imaginary boxes on your canvas and finding a nice composition and balance. The next step is to add more details to the boxes by playing with subtraction, addition, or intersection of volumes.

The focus of this exercise is on full understanding of the perspective rules, composition, and your spatial imagination during sketching.

The focus is not on scale or realism, so you are free to experiment. Give it a couple of tries to find the right balance in your image. Again, you are encouraged to get inspired by a movie, a poster, or whatever you find relevant. Have fun!

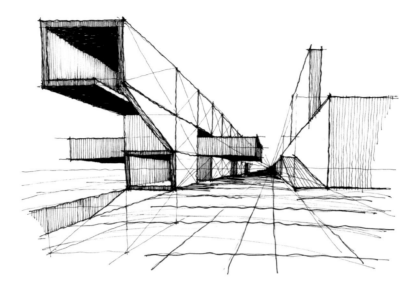

1-Point Perspective sketch evoking modular architecture

TIP

Start with small and quick thumbnail sketches to test different ideas of a sketched composition.

Follow any composition rules of your choice (the golden rule, rule of thirds, etc.) to guide you when placing volumes in perspective.

Always begin by drawing imaginary boxes first. Detailing and hatching comes later.

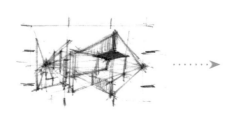

Thumbnail sketch suggesting a composition

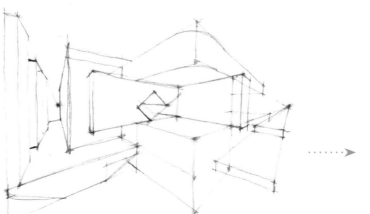

Pencil sketch - testing proportions and detailing the volumes

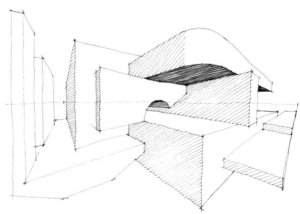

Clean pen sketch of an abstract volumetric composition (tracing paper)

Step 02

Wrap up

Here's a wrap up of the main tips and tricks for sketching perspectives. These advice should serve as guidelines, but feel free to use what suits you the best and leave the rest out with no worries.

#01
Start with a thumbnail sketch to test your ideas and compositions.

#02
Always draw imaginary boxes first and then the objects inside these boxes.

#03
Make use of design principles such as repetition, balance, and contrast.

#04
Create dynamics in your sketch by sketching long diagonal lines.

#05
Follow composition rules such as the golden rule, rule of thirds or others.

#06
Play with volumes by subtracting, adding, or intersecting them.

Step 03

Shadows, Textures & Materiality

Now that we are confident about lines, 2D objects, and perspective sketching, we are ready to move on. To improve our sketches, we need to add more details, specifically by working with light and shadows and by expressing materiality through different textures.

In this chapter, we will start by defining shade and shadow and sketching different lighting conditions in perspective to add more plasticity and depth to our drawings.

Subsequently, you will learn how to visually represent materials in your sketch, such as brick, stone, concrete, timber, or glass.

To create suggestive textures, we'll take inspiration from real-life references, simplify them to textures, and sketch them through various rendering techniques. Let's get started!

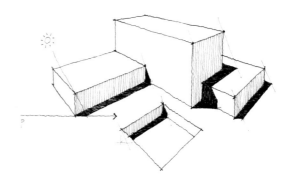

Shade and Shadow

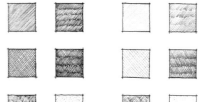

Rendering Techniques

Shade and Shadow

In order to create a convincing perspective sketch with volumetric qualities, we should add correct shadows to our spatial composition.

First, we define the light source (sun, bulb etc.). In architectural sketches we choose the position of the light source with a certain intention to enhance the spatial qualities of our sketch.

The brightness of the surfaces of our object are effected by the light source - exposed surfaces are brighter, sheltered surfaces are darker.

Furthermore, there are two kinds of shadows - **cast shadow (shadow)** and **form shadow (shade)**.

A **shadow** is the silhouette cast by an object that blocks a source of light. A **shade** is the less defined dark side of an object not facing the light source.

Use Worksheet 03.a on the next page to practice Shade and Shadow!

THE IMPORTANT RULE for our drawing is that a Shadow is always darker than a Shade.

TIP

In this explanatory sketch, a bulb produces a cone of light. In other examples using sunlight, Sun rays might be considered parallel because of the great distance of the Sun (Worksheet 03.a).

Light Source (e.g. a bulb)

Real Direction of the Light Ray

VP1

Horizon Line

VP2

Plan Position of Light Source (up to an artist to choose it to achieve the desired shading effect)

Direction of the Light Ray in Plan

Parallel lines converging at the same Vanishing Point.

Shade (Form Shadow)

Shadow (Cast Shadow)

WORKSHEET 03.a

This Worksheet is for practicing correct shading technique by adding a shade and a shadow to the composition.

To do so, follow the chosen **Real Direction of Sunlight** (the diagonal line with the sign of Sun, defined through the corner of one of the objects) and its **Direction in Plan** (the horizontal arrow with a letter "p").

In this case, consider the sun rays parallel - the Real Direction of Sunlight will have the same orientation in the whole composition.

If in doubt, check the first page of this chapter (p. 32) to see the correct shading solution for this Worksheet.

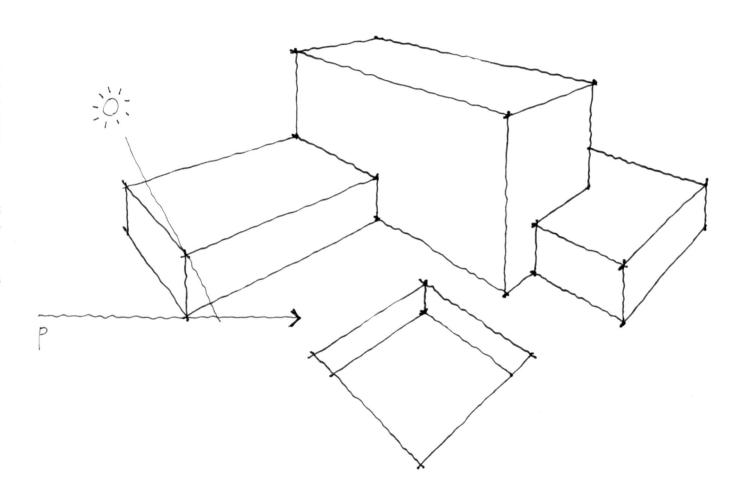

P

Rendering Techniques

Mastering rendering techniques is massively important to ensure a high quality sketch. The effect of these techniques depends on a rendering medium and on a chosen paper and its texture.

In the examples on the right hand side of this page, you can see the differences between a pen with 0.1 tip and a pencil with graphite hardness 2B.

The pen lines are sharper in comparison to the pencil. However, the pen is not capable of drawing dynamic strokes, so there are almost no differences in the thickness of lines or tone values.

The pencil, on the other hand, is a softer medium than a pen and artists can vary the strokes depending on the level of pressure applied. Because of that, in my opinion, it takes more effort and experience to truly master pencil drawing techniques.

By practicing, you should understand the differences in the use of rendering mediums and papers together with appropriate techniques to achieve the desired impact in a sketch.

Hatching (Separate Lines)   Hatching (Continuous Lines)   Hatching (Separate Lines)   Hatching (Continuous Lines)

Cross Hatching (Separate Lines)   Cross Hatching (Continuous Lines)   Cross Hatching (Separate Lines)   Cross Hatching (Continuous Lines)

Pattern   Pointilism   Pattern   Pointilism

Textures & Materiality

Now we are going to use the rende-ring techniques mentioned before to create suggestive textures expressing materiality in our objects.

In these examples you can see the most common materials which we depict in architectural sketches.

Some of the textures, e.g. stone or timber, might be used for different elements in a space, such as walls, floors/roads, beams etc. That being said, we should always try to adjust these textures so they fit their con-text - by means of correct perspec-tive and the level of detail.

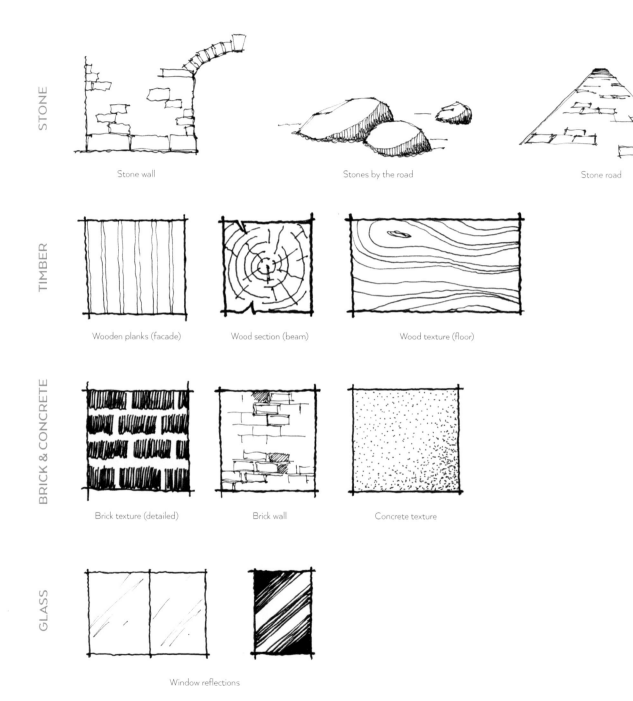

STONE

Stone wall   Stones by the road   Stone road

TIMBER

Wooden planks (facade)   Wood section (beam)   Wood texture (floor)

BRICK & CONCRETE

Brick texture (detailed)   Brick wall   Concrete texture

GLASS

Window reflections

WORKSHEET 03.b

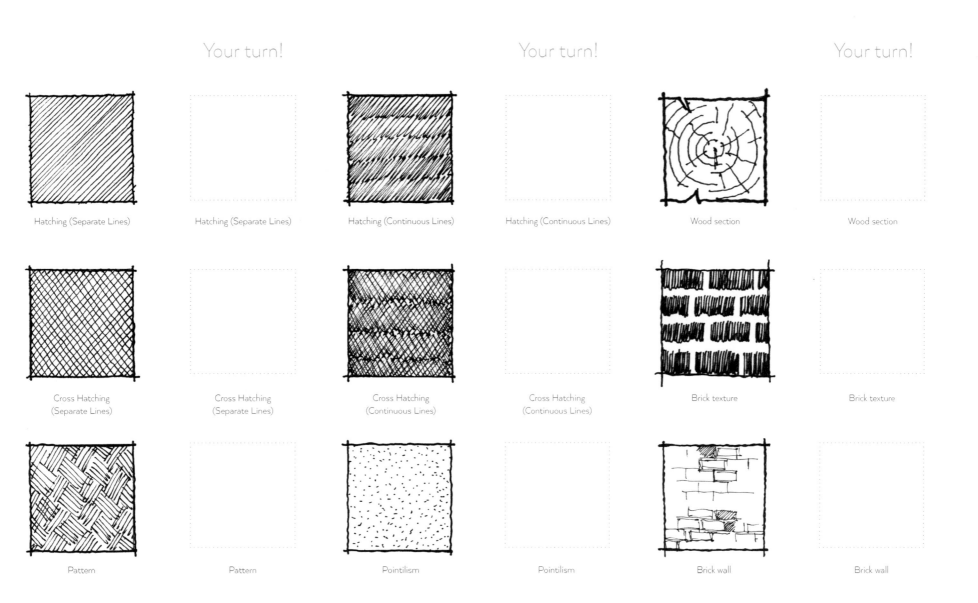

Your turn!

Your turn!

Your turn!

Hatching (Separate Lines)

Hatching (Separate Lines)

Hatching (Continuous Lines)

Hatching (Continuous Lines)

Wood section

Wood section

Cross Hatching
(Separate Lines)

Cross Hatching
(Separate Lines)

Cross Hatching
(Continuous Lines)

Cross Hatching
(Continuous Lines)

Brick texture

Brick texture

Pattern

Pattern

Pointilism

Pointilism

Brick wall

Brick wall

Exercise

This time the exercise will be even more fun to do. For practicing various texturing techniques and suggesting materiality in your sketch, I prepared a perspective composition without any textures. **Your task is to finish the sketch by adding all the details.**

Although the main focus here is on applying textures, feel free to add more details in perspective such as windows or railings. You can also add more volumes or play with the composition as you like. Again, feel free to experiment!

Make use of different lineweights, put city silhouettes on the horizon, draw jagged lines to suggest foliage, or get creative with the sky. Try to add different kinds of details to spice up this basic composition.

Use Worksheet 03.c on the next page or draw your own perspective composition. Make use of all the experience you have and you've gained so far to finish the image. Happy sketching!

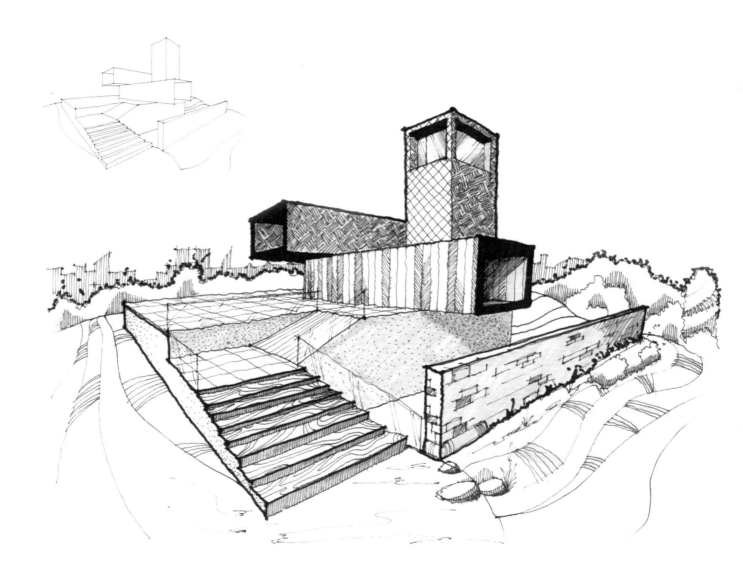

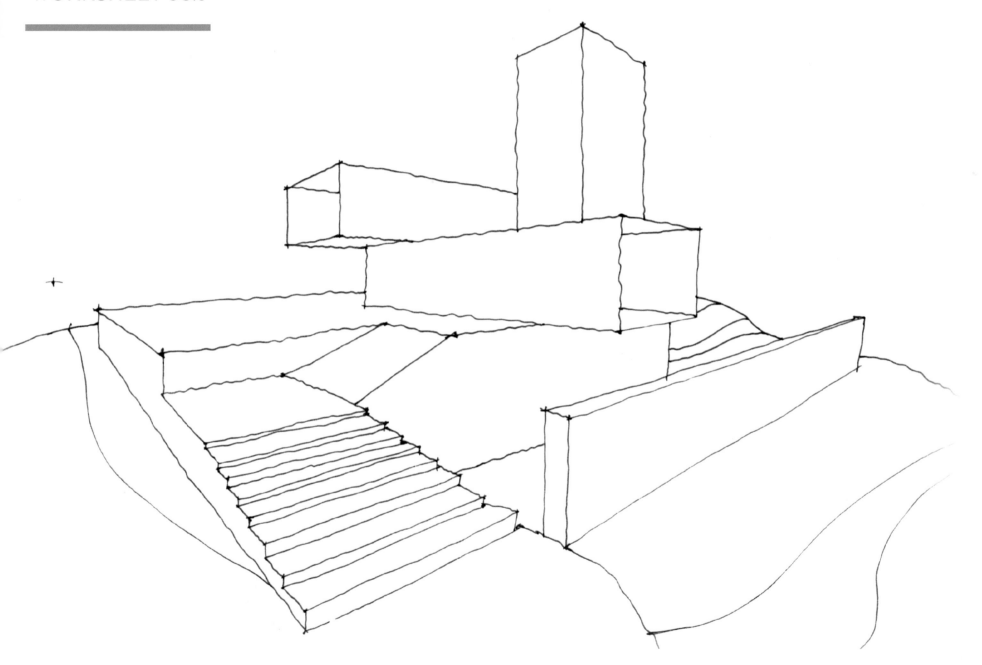

Step 03

Wrap up

I believe that by now you've learned how massively the texturing & shading affect the final result. It might be a bit tedious sometimes but it's definitely worth it! Here again is a summary of the most important tips.

#01
Shading - shadow is always darker than shade.

#02
Textures work as a graphic simplification suggesting real-life materials.

#03
Make use of selective texturing - highlight only some areas.

#04
Define the Real Direction of Light, coming always through a corner of an object.

#05
Learn the differences between using a pen and a pencil for shading and texturing.

#06
Observe your surroundings to get a correct understanding of light and shadows.

Step 04

Populating Your Sketch

At this stage, we move forward to sketching human figures as it is an essential skill in order to better understand a sketched space. There are several reasons why integrating human figures in architectural sketches is important.

Generally speaking, architecture is about creating spaces for people. From this point of view, it makes sense to add people into spaces which are meant for them. By doing so, we depict more lively environments and we create greater opportunities to express our idea, because people are the key element of storytelling.

Finally, and most importantly, human figures add a sense of scale to our sketches. Therefore, we should always refer to a human figure when defining the scale of sketched spaces and surroundings.

In this chapter, we will learn a quick way how to sketch human figures based on the right proportions, how to incorporate them into perspective sketches, and how to work with them to build a sketched composition in the right scale.

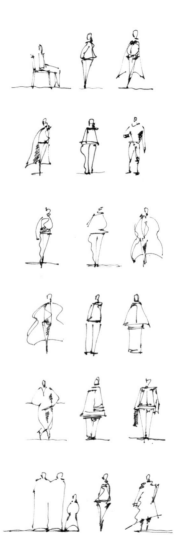

Quickly Sketched Human Figures

Human Figures

When quickly sketching human figures, we use loose curves and more dynamic strokes. The important aspect of such drawing is the proportions. By keeping the right proportions, we make sure that our sketch evokes human figures, or even better - looks realistic. To support this, it is also recommended to draw the ground the figure is standing on, or the figure's cast shadow, so it doesn't seem like people are flying in the air.

We usually draw all figures with more or less the same relative height (as seen in the examples on this page). Another case is sketching sitting people or children - their height must be adjusted accordingly.

As always, the level of detail matters - sometimes just a curve or silhouette contour will do fine, sometimes you add more clothing details, a suitcase in hand etc.

It is a good idea to draw groups of people instead of a number of individuals - suggesting an interaction between them builds a foundation for storytelling in our image.

WORKSHEET 04.a

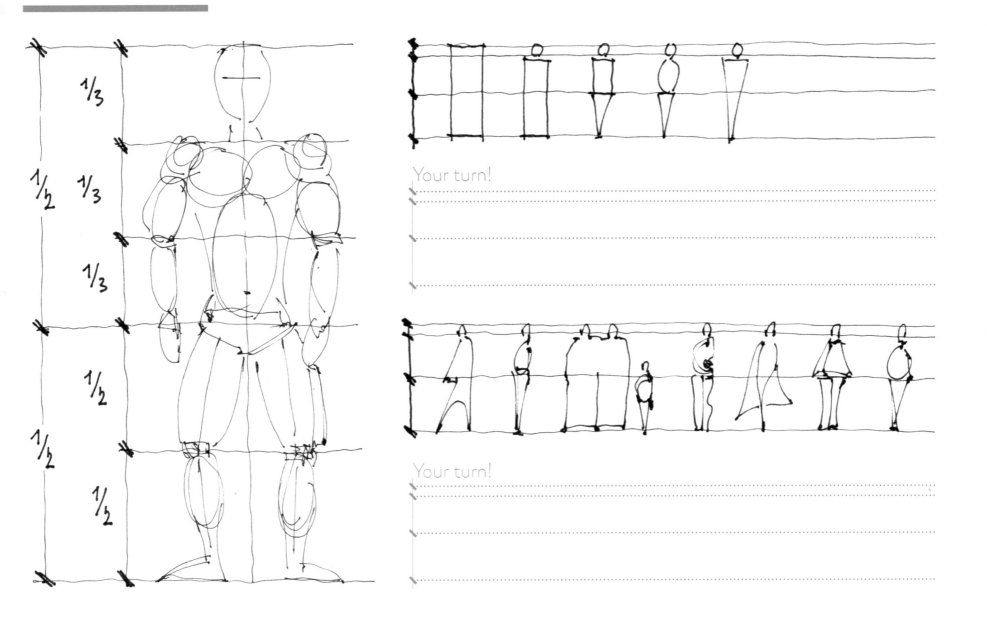

⅓

½ ⅓

⅓

½

½

Your turn!

Your turn!

Exercise

Your Exercise for practicing populating your sketch is to **sketch a composition of human figures in an eye-level perspective.**

For start, you can suggest a simple spatial setting in an eye-level perspective to put your figures into. In the example on the right hand side, I chose to sketch a space evoking a public plaza, so a number of differently distributed people would feel natural in there.

When you're done outlining the spatial setting, add 10 to 15 figures in various depth layers to your sketch. The rule number one for populating your eye-level perspective sketch is to keep every figure's head on the horizon. We assume that all of them would be the same height (except for children or sitting people).

Also keep in mind the composition of an image. Note, for example, how the main building is graphically balanced with the closest figure in the foreground.

Happy sketching!

Step 04

Wrap up

As usual, here's a wrap up of the main tips and tricks, this time for sketching human figures. These advice should serve as guidelines, but feel free to use what suits you the best and leave the rest out with no worries.

#01
Use loose curves and more dynamic strokes to quickly sketch human figures.

#02
Keep the right proportions between head, body, and legs to achieve a realistic look.

#03
Use human figures to determine scale and depth in your image.

#04
To suggest interaction, draw groups of people instead of a number of individuals.

#05
In an eye-level perspective, draw all the standing people's heads on the horizon line.

#06
Draw the ground a figure is standing on, or a cast shadow, so it doesn't look like people are flying in the air.

Step 05

Adding Vegetation

As a final step before putting everything together, we'll take a look at vegetation as an element in architectural sketching.

Natural elements can play an important role in any visuals. Through combining (very often) boxy architecture with more organic shapes of vegetation, we can achieve a very appealing image. Moreover, vegetation might serve well for defining a setting for our image, for framing the spectator's view, and unveiling the real focal point of an image.

That being said, vegetation is a very powerful and universal element to use in sketches. In this chapter we'll focus on drawing trees, bushes, and grass in different scales and from different angles. Let's dive into it!

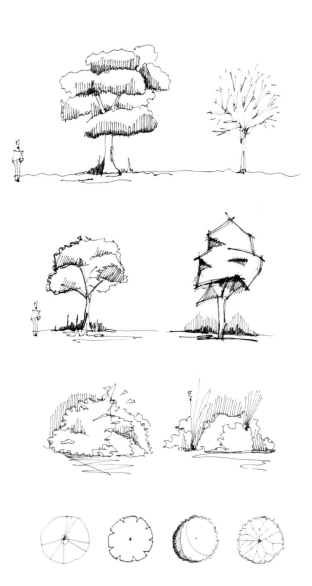

Variations on sketched trees and bushes

Vegetation

As you can see from the examples on this page, drawing vegetation does not require anything new from us. We still use lines and 2D objects, just in a slightly different manner.

Since we graphically suggest something natural and organic, it should be also reflected in the style of our lines and 2D objects. To be specific, it means that we use jagged lines, irregular shapes, uneven distribution of elements, and generally a more free-hand style of sketching.

Take time to study examples on the next two pages and notice how the sketching techniques from previous chapters were applied to the sketched vegetation - various line types, hatching & shading techniques, use of lineweight, etc.

Examples of sketched grass

Examples of sketched bushes

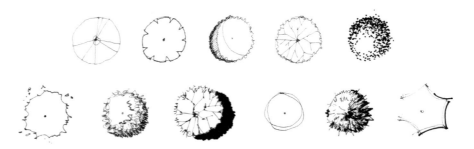

Various styles of trees from a top view

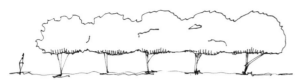

A group of trees in small scale (in distance) is perceived as one coherent volume.

On this page you can see a number of examples of trees which differ in their scale and level of detail.

As a rule of thumb, I recommend drawing the trunk of a grown tree at least the same height as a human figure.

In case of more detailed trees, it is a good idea to add grass or bushes in the area where a trunk meets the ground. It makes a tree well-placed.

TIP

Note how the scale, defined by a human figure, influences the level of detail applied to the sketched trees.

Examples of simply sketched trees derived from basic 2D shapes.

Examples of trees with higher level of detail.

WORKSHEET 05.a

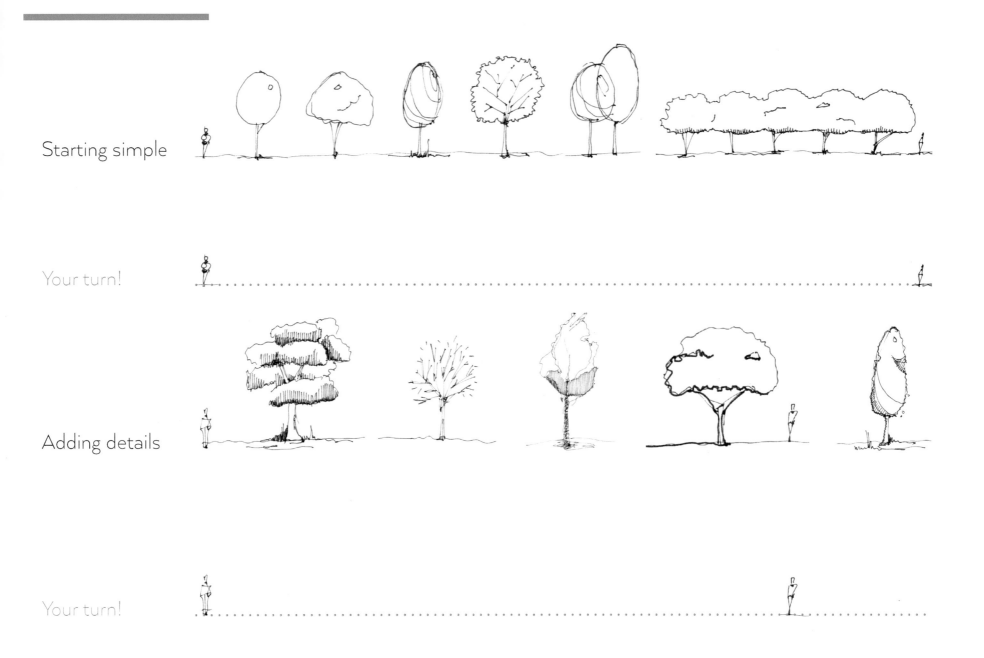

Starting simple

Your turn!

Adding details

Your turn!

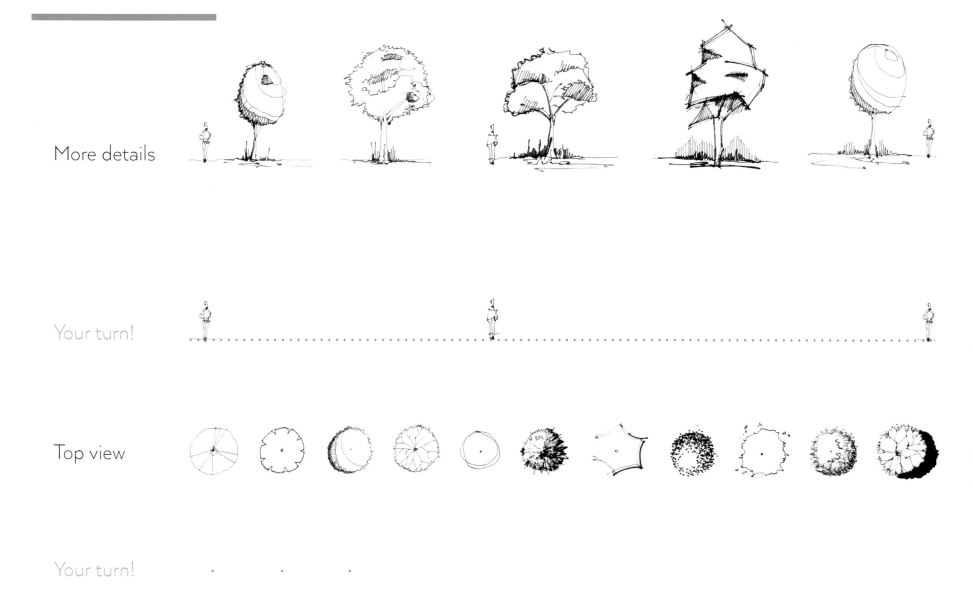

More details

Your turn!

Top view

Your turn!

Inspiration

There are endless ways how to draw trees and vegetation. Use these sketches as a source of your inspiration and experiment with your own style!

Foliage 01

Foliage 02

Gradient Hatching

Grass

Linear/ Cross Hatching

Exercise

This time it is a quick and fun exercise for practicing vegetation. **Your task is to sketch a simple scene with different types of vegetation, including at least 2-3 trees, some bushes, and grass.**

You should start by defining the scale with a human figure and then drawing a basic composition of trees. In the examples on the right hand side, there is always one small and one big tree, but you are free to choose your own composition.

Subsequently, you complement the sketch with smaller elements, such as small pots with flowers, bushes, and grass.

As a final touch, I recommend to anchor the composition by defining a setting - in this case, a simple brick wall in the background will do fine.

Don't forget to use your knowledge from previous chapters and thus make use of lineweight to add emphasis and contrast to your sketch, or use shading techniques to suggest volume of vegetation.

Good luck!

Step 05

Wrap up

Here's a wrap up of the main tips and tricks for sketching vegetation. These advice should serve as guidelines, but feel free to use what suits you the best and leave the rest out with no worries.

#01
For vegetation, we use jagged lines, irregular shapes, and generally a free-hand style of sketching.

#02
Level of the detail applied to vegetation depends on its scale (distance from a viewer).

#03
Simplify the trees which are in the distance and apply more details to the trees in the foreground.

#04
Draw the trunk of a grown tree at least the same height as a human figure.

#05
In case of more detailed trees, add grass or bushes in the area where the trunk meets the ground.

#06
Vegetation serves well for defining a setting, framing a view, or unveiling the focal point of an image.

Step 06

Awesome Perspective Sketch

In this last chapter, we'll have a look at ways to combine all of the previous elements into an awesome perspective sketch. The focus will be on integrating them in a way so we achieve the desired impact – specific mood, atmosphere, or story in a sketch.

With this final exercise, the goal is to learn how to translate this impact into a sketch by working with composition, scale, depth planes, and focal points.

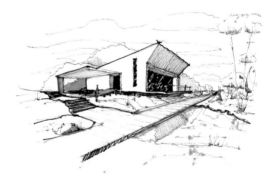

One of the important aspects and variables is also whether we draw from our imagination or by observing an existing reference. Here you'll have a chance to study different examples of finished sketches, describing key techniques and explaining the workflow behind an image.

On the next pages, you can follow the tips on each sketch to get some insight into the chosen techniques and approaches. Happy sketching!

Exercise

Your final task is to create at least one free-hand perspective sketch and use all the skills and knowledge you've obtained so far. The type of perspective is up to you, as well as the source of your inspiration - you can draw either from observation or from your imagination.

A good idea is to choose your favourite building or a building from your favourite architect, if you have one. It actually doesn't need to be a whole building, but it can be a small part of it or just an interesting detail.

Once you decide on the subject, I recommend creating a clear vision of what the final image should look like. It might help to answer questions like - **What do I want to show in this picture? What is the most important thing about this building? Where do I want the viewers to look first? What story should the image tell?**

Give it some thought, but most importantly, do it! Allow yourself to experiment, sketch several ideas and find out what suits you the best. Your unique human touch to a sketch is very often the most precious added value. Feel free to refer back to previous chapters and practice a specific technique if needed. Happy sketching!

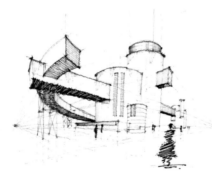

One of the possible workflows might go like this:

- testing ideas on small thumbnail sketches
- choosing a good composition
- establishing the right scale with a human figure
- drawing a focal area (imaginary boxes first)
- adding surroundings, more people, vegetation
- adding more details, hatches, shading, and colour

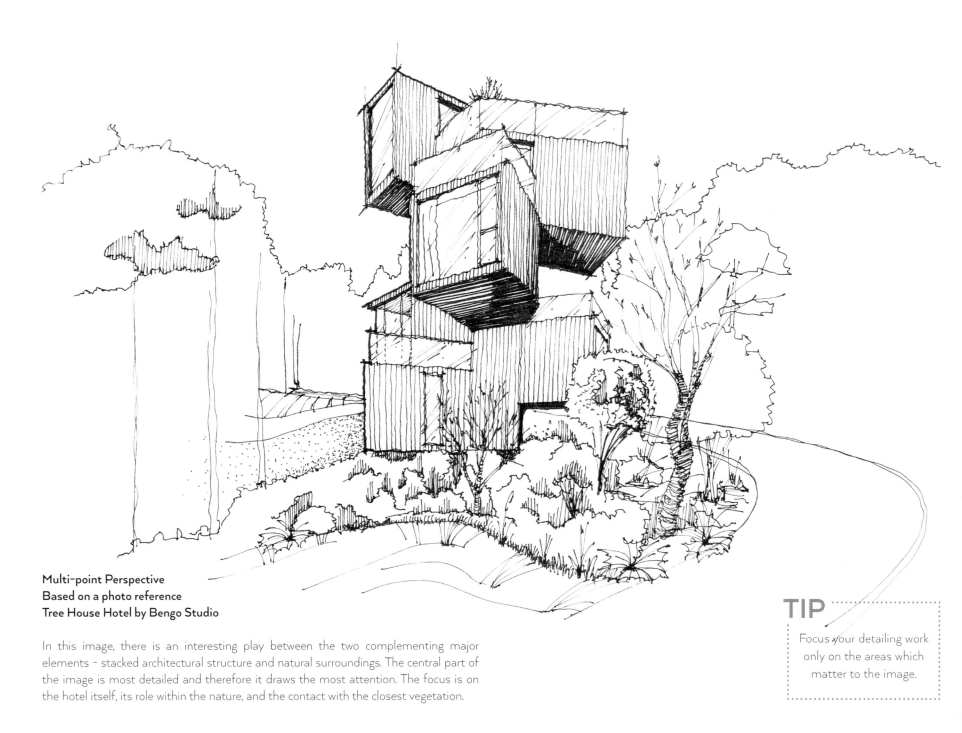

Multi-point Perspective
Based on a photo reference
Tree House Hotel by Bengo Studio

In this image, there is an interesting play between the two complementing major elements - stacked architectural structure and natural surroundings. The central part of the image is most detailed and therefore it draws the most attention. The focus is on the hotel itself, its role within the nature, and the contact with the closest vegetation.

TIP
Focus your detailing work only on the areas which matter to the image.

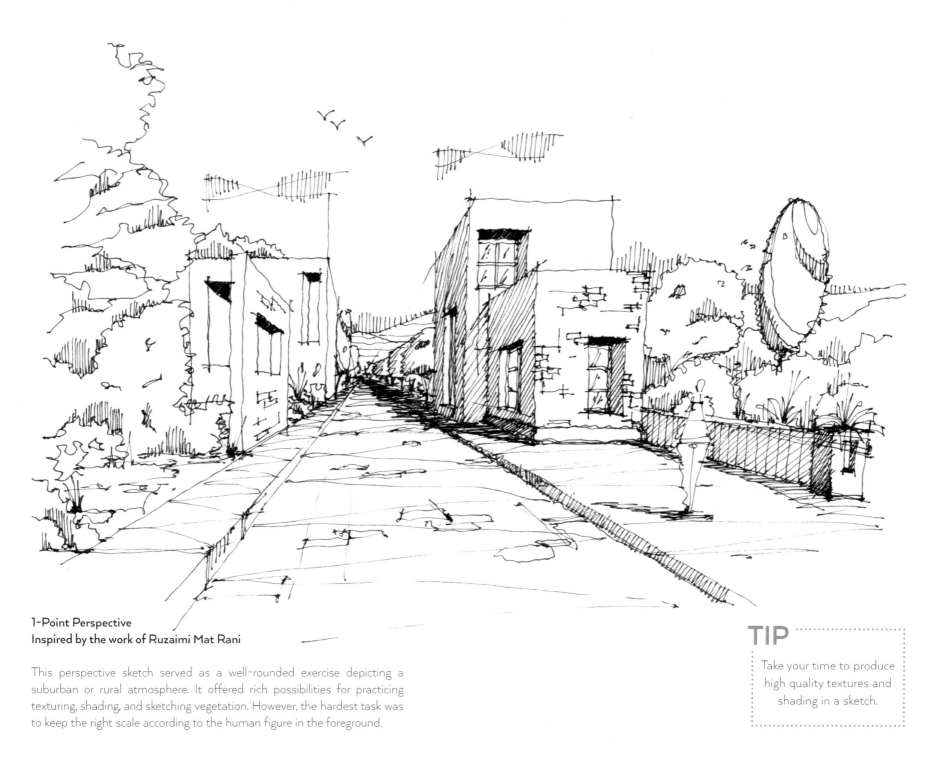

1-Point Perspective
Inspired by the work of Ruzaimi Mat Rani

This perspective sketch served as a well-rounded exercise depicting a suburban or rural atmosphere. It offered rich possibilities for practicing texturing, shading, and sketching vegetation. However, the hardest task was to keep the right scale according to the human figure in the foreground.

2-Point Perspective (Vertical)
Imagination

This image offers an unusual look at 2-Point Perspective. The Horizon Lines is positioned vertically on the axis of the drawing. The first Vanishing Point lies at the bottom of the door, whereas the other Vanishing Point is positioned high above the top of the building. Such use of 2-Point Perspective can suplement some aspects of 3-Point Perspective. This arrangement allows for a strong expression of verticality and complements the geometry of the high-rise building.

TIP

Think of how you
can complement
a building's geometry
in your composition.

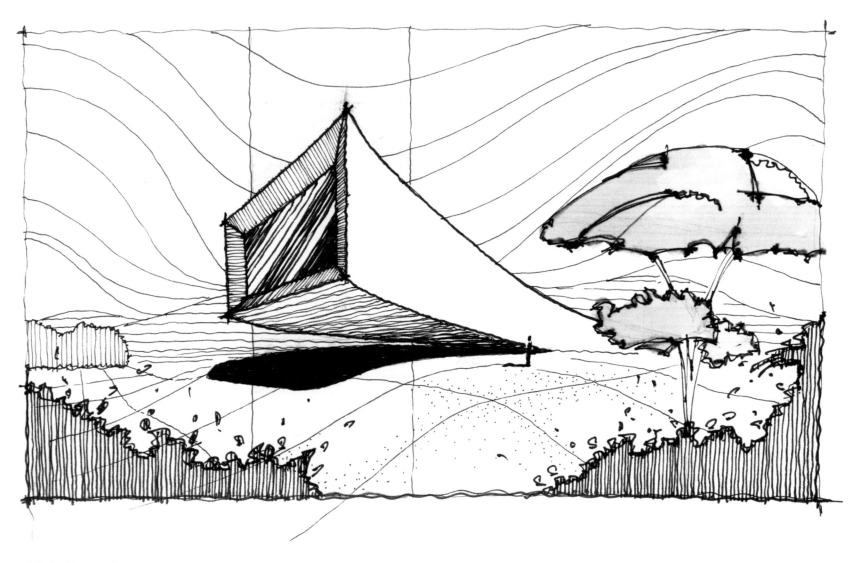

2-Point Perspective
Imagination

This image was a really good exercise for perspective and composition. To add a sense of depth, I was working with the 3 depth planes – foreground, middle ground, and background. At the end, I emphasized the focal point with a colour accent. This time I also tried a bit more creative approach to the sky which supports the flow of the building and the landscape.

TIP

Get creative with graphic ideas for the sky!

2-Point Perspective
Imagination

Lonely, quiet, calm – I had these three values in mind when creating this image.
Instead of a busy city context, a simple summer house is placed in a very natural
environment, offering peace of mind. All the natural elements are very important
to the desired atmosphere, including the water with reflections. As a final touch,
I used a colour marker to enhance the shading of the image.

TIP

Try adding some water
elements to your composition!

Multi-Point Perspective
Based on a photo reference
Copenhagen in Detail

Since I like to walk through the streets
of old cities and observe buildings,
I took some photos in Copenhagen as
references for sketching. This sketch
depicts the lower half of an oriel of a
5-storey building in Østerbro.

As the scale of the sketch is big, it
requires a high level of detail. That
is a very challenging change from
regular exterior sketches. Nonetheless,
I encourage you to pay attention to
such small details - on the buildings,
on the streets, or in a public space
in general. Very often you need to
thoroughly understand the principle
behind a detail and its tectonic
qualities in order to sketch it properly.

This was a great exercise in observation
skills and detailing work, including
window reflections and shading
techniques.

TIP

Pay attention to small details
and practice observation.

1-Point Perspective
Based on a photo reference

The idea behind this image was to showcase a linear exhibition pavilion in nature. The geometry of the pavilion here allows for strong diagonals which creates dynamics and depth in the sketch. To enhance the natural context, the foreground is outlined by a tree and bushes, framing the whole image.

TIP

Think creatively about framing your image!

2-Point Perspective
Expandable House in Indonesia
by Urban Rural Systems
Based on a photo reference

Similarly to the sketch on the left facing page, vegetation and framing play key roles in presenting the settings of this sustainable project.

Apart from showing the context, the framing adds more depth as well as visual interest to the sketch.

Try to always analyze various image elements - the really necessary ones play important part both in a content (subject, message, idea) and a form (composition, visual principles) of an image.

TIP ·················

Necessary visual elements play a key role both in a content and a form of an image.

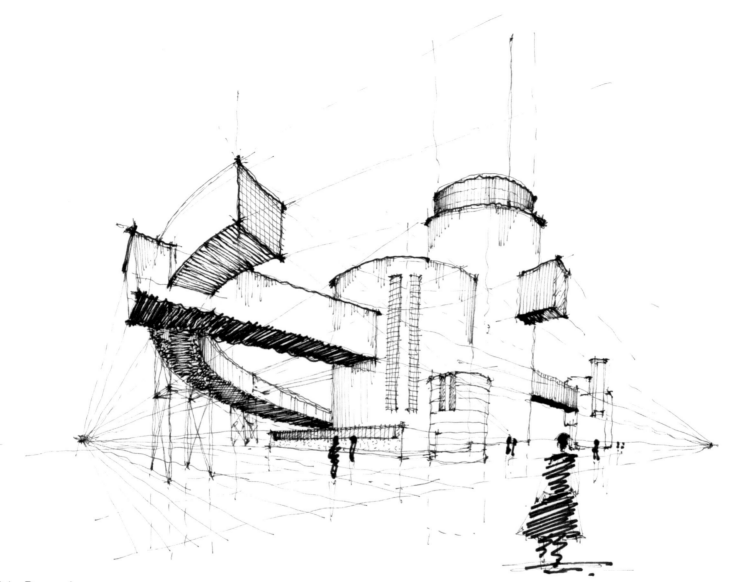

Multi-Point Perspective
Imagination

Industrial theme was in my mind when sketching this image. It served mainly as an exercise in composition and multi-point perspective. Notice there are 3 main volumes in the composition - 2 overlapping cylinders and one circular pathway, all of them perforated with a linear horizontal volume complementing the vertical ones. Number 3 and other odd numbers of elements work well when setting up your compositions (the Rule of Odds).

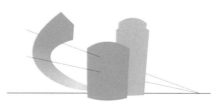

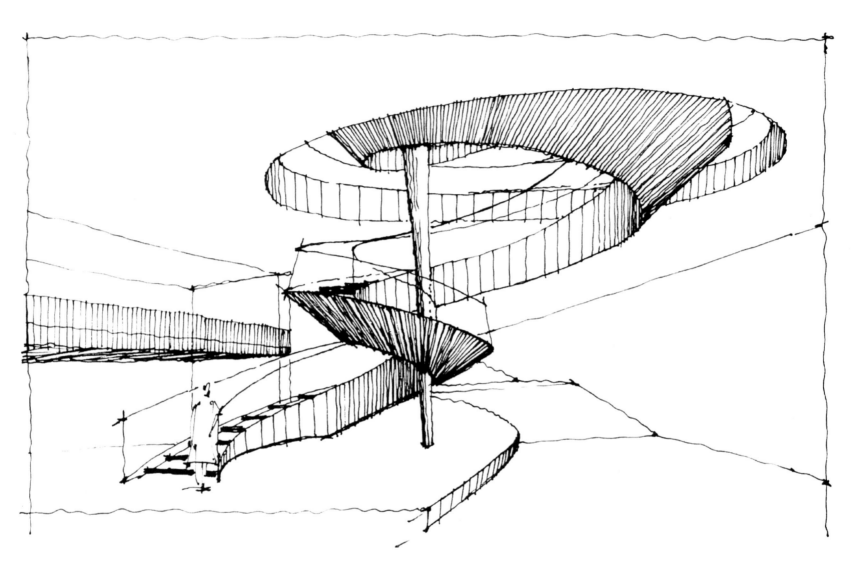

Multi-Point Perspective
Antinori Winery in Tuscany, Italy
by Archea Associati
Based on a photo reference

Probably the most beautiful staircase I've had the chance to see with my own eyes so far.
Incredible form and and very elegant structure! The crucial part of the sketching process was
getting the proportions right. I drew just from observation without any complicated structures
behind the form - first in pencil, then in ink.

TIP

Outline more complex
forms with a pencil first,
then finish it with ink.

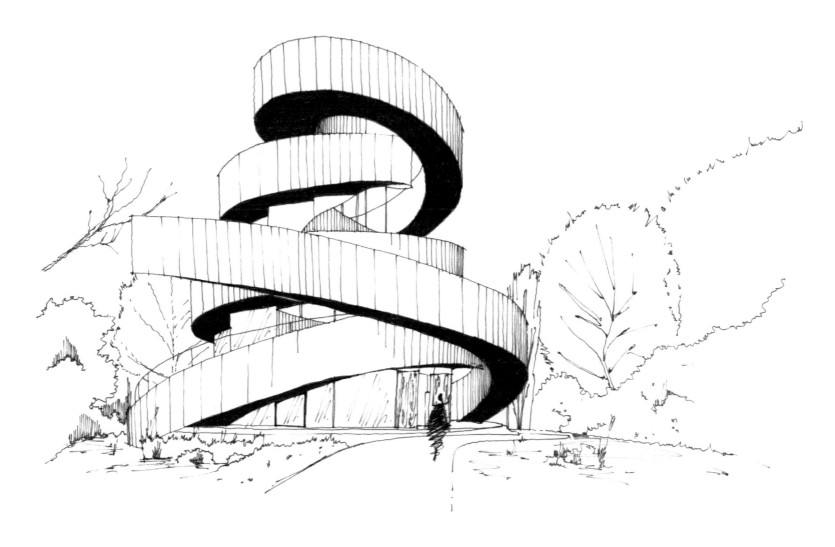

Multi-Point Perspective
Ribbon Chapel in Hiroshima, Japan
by Hiroshi Nakamura & NAP
Based on a photo reference

One has to love this wedding chapel based on two entwining spiral stairways, supporting each other both literally (structural support) and figuratively (as two people in a marriage). Its form and its meaning were the motivation behind my sketch. You can notice more detail and higher contrast on the building itself, focusing the viewer's eyes on the iconic form.

TIP
Use higher contrast and detail to drive attention towards focal areas of an image.

Multi-Point Perspective
Guggenheim Museum in New York City
by Frank Lloyd Wright
Based on a photo reference

One of the classics in modern architecture which I've had the chance to visit in person. The iconic form speaks for itself. I intentionally left out some of the surrounding volumes to get clearer outline of this masterpiece.

TIP

Get clarity on what you want to show in a sketch.

Step 06

Wrap up

You know the drill by now. Here are the final tips & tricks for achieving awesome perspective sketches. Take them easy, customize them, or come up with your own guidelines.

#01
Focus your detailing work only on the areas which matter to the image.

#02
Take your time to produce high quality textures and shading in a sketch.

#03
Think of how you can complement a building's geometry in your composition.

#04
Get creative with graphic ideas for the sky!

#05
Try adding some water elements to your composition!

#06
Pay attention to small details and practice observation.

#07
Think creatively about framing your image!

#08
Use colour accents to emphasize certain areas or shapes in your sketch.

Conclusion

Big congratulations for making it so far! I really hope you enjoyed the journey, learned new things about sketching, and put some of the tips and techniques to good use. However, this is not the end.

If there is one thing I'd like you to take with you, it would be this: Remember that imperfections are what make free-hand sketching so unique. The human touch plays a key role in architectural sketching and everyone can find his or her own style, so there is no right or wrong approach. Be open, experiment a lot, stay humble, and keep practicing!

I'll be happy if you found some bits and pieces from this book useful, and I would definitely appreciate your feedback, so feel free to drop me a line on my website or via social media. Thanks!

Happy sketching!

Thoughts On Drawing

NO RULERS PLEASE

I really prefer not to use rulers, because free-hand sketching brings so much more freedom to both sketching process and the dialogue that evolves from it. I perceive sketching as a means of communication more than anything else. And free-hand sketching with wavy imperfect lines leaves a lot of space for opening a creative dialogue - either between colleagues, or an architect and a client. The imperfections suggest that nothing is set in stone and that everybody is welcome to contribute with their own inputs.

HUMAN TOUCH

I can't imagine something would replace hand-sketching in our industries in any foreseeable future. I believe it will stay an important part of both design process and presentation and maybe there will be even more demand for it as the human touch added to hand-renderings is irreplaceable and will always connect us on a very human level.

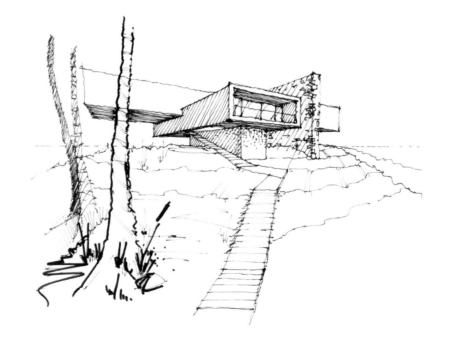

ABOUT INSPIRATION

As for sources of inspiration, I believe that architects shouldn't get inspired by another architecture – that's very limiting. Don't get me wrong, it's important to do research and moodboards with reference pictures, but that's not inspiration in true sense. In regards to this, there is one quote from architect Edmund Bacon that really resonates with me. He says: "It's in the doing that the idea comes." It really does work like that for me – I get ideas during the process, very often as I sketch, because there are no barriers as with using a software on a computer. The connection between your mind and your hand is very natural and it supports all the creative flows.

"*It's in the doing
that the idea comes.*"
~ Edmund Bacon, architect & urban planner

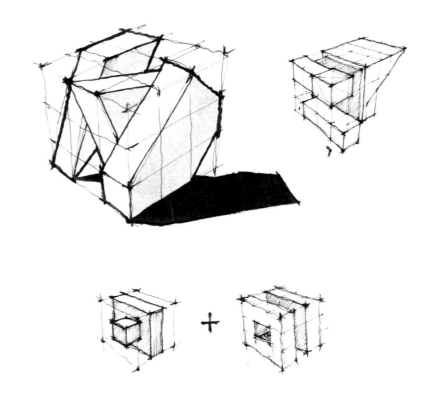

THE SKETCHING PROCESS

The process differs according to the type of sketch. There are many types, most of them are for communicating ideas, but some process sketches are simply for brainstorming, trying to understand a problem and come up with a solution, or for further shaping and verifying ideas that emerge on the way. If we talk about presentation sketches, I like to start with a thumbnail sketch where I first try to find the best composition in terms of relations between different elements and positioning on a canvas. Depending on complexity, I begin either with a pencil or a pen to create a visual structure and set the right scale. Then I use pens with lighter line weight to build up the main volumes and work with different depth planes. I continue with texturing and shading, adding more of surroundings and details. Final touches might include line work with heavier line weight for emphasis and contrast or optionally use of colour.

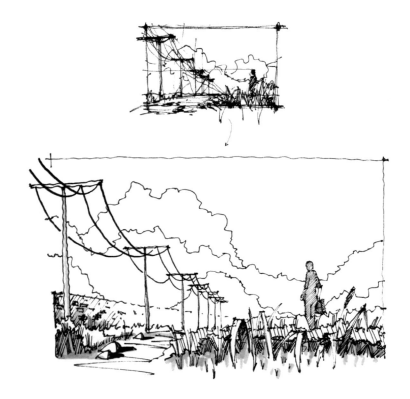

WHY WAVY LINES?

Adding a little squiggle to your lines or making them wavy instead of razor-straight makes the lines less perfect and more human. When you draw all the lines like that in a drawing, it creates a really sketchy impression - and that might be a good thing! It tells a viewer (your colleague or a client) that you're open to discussion. By that you invite them to participate in the process and you start a dialogue instead of one-way communication.

ONE TIP ABOVE ALL

If I should choose just one thing that is often neglected but has dramatic impact on your sketches - it's your observation skills. Learn to observe and understand why things work and look like they do. Observation skills are essential for good sketching, for composition, light and shadows, proportions, materiality, and everything else. Train yourself to be better at observing positive and negative space of objects, their proportions, and spatial relations between them! It's a skill like any other and with a little bit of practice, you'll get better and, more importantly, your sketches will improve. What I love about sketching is that it forces you to understand the object first before you're able to draw it. In that way, when you sketch you'll always learn something new.

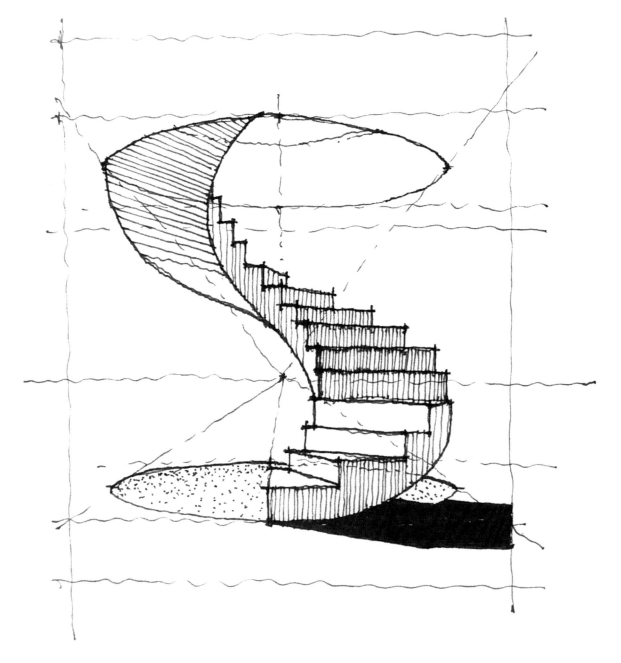

Next Steps

Now that you've finished all the steps, the fun doesn't have to stop. Here are some suggestions on what you can do next to squeeze the most out of this book.

First, head over to **SketchLikeAnArchitect.com/ReadersOnly** and download all the printable Worksheets from this book so you never run out of resources for practicing.

On the webpage you'll also find links to extra resources for your inspiration in the form of videos, blog posts, and other downloadables.

If you already have sketches to share, post them on social media with the hashtag #SketchLikeAnArchitect and tag me - I'll be happy to give you a shoutout and send your posts some love.

Please, leave an honest review on Amazon.com (or any other online book retailer you bought this book from).

Finally, join me in the corresponding online video course where I'll personally walk you through all the exercises, demonstrate the techniques covered in this book, and give you feedback on your sketches. Again, visit **SketchLikeAnArchitect.com/ReadersOnly** for a special link to the course.

References and Resources to Explore

Here is a list of the references used when creating this Handbook and resources you might find valuable and inspiring to further explore.

Publications

- Dease, Carole, and collective, *Complete Drawing Course*, London, 2001,
- Rani, Ruzaimi Mat, *Sketching Masterclass*, Singapore, 2010,
- Stanyer, Peter, *The Complete Book of Drawing Techniques*, London, 2004,
- Sýkora, Jaroslav a kolektiv, *Architektonické kreslení*, Praha, 2003,
- Wilk, Sabrina, *Construction and Design Manual - Drawing for Landscape Architects*, Berlin, 2014.

Online Resources to Explore

- Online Course corresponding to this Handbook: SketchLikeAnArchitect.Teachable.com
- Download and print all the Worksheets for practicing from this book here: www.SketchLikeAnArchitect.com/ReadersOnly
- Download all the related Freebies here: www.SketchLikeAnArchitect.com/Freebies

Sketching App for Practicing

- ShadowDraw - download the ShadowDraw app on your iPad and practice sketching with my stroke-by-stroke tutorials.

SKETCH
Like an Architect

In today's world focused on technology, we sometimes forget how such simple tools as pen and paper can help us brainstorm and communicate ideas, quickly iterate a design, solve a problem, or simply understand a perceived object or our own thoughts.

The mission of the Sketch Like an Architect project is to share values and benefits of hand-sketching for architects, designers, and hobby sketchers and to provide high-quality resources for further learning and improvement in this area.

About the Author

David Drazil, MSc.
- Young Architect Who Loves to Sketch
- Online Teacher, Author, External Lecturer
- Founder of SketchLikeAnArchitect.com

David Drazil is a young architect, who loves to sketch. With passion for visual presentation of architecture, he's sharing freebies and educational resources on how to #SketchLikeAnArchitect.

Since his childhood he's been fascinated by visuals and has been inclined to fine arts, architecture, and graphic design. During his architectural studies, both in the Czech Republic and Denmark, David found his passion in the visual presentation of architecture - namely architectural sketching, visualisations, animation, and virtual reality.

David gained international experience while studying at Aalborg University and working as an architect for KHR Architects and Danielsen Architecture in Copenhagen, Denmark.

Today, David is focused on helping architects, designers, and hobby sketchers to use sketching as a tool for better design process and presentation. He's also collaborating as a featured artist with sketching apps on iPad called ShadowDraw and Morpholio Trace.

Find more information on the website SketchLikeAnArchitect.com or at David's successful Instagram account (@david_drazil) where he shares daily his tips & tricks on how to #SketchLikeAnArchitect.

Find out more about David and the #SketchLikeAnArchitect project:

🌐 SketchLikeAnArchitect.com

📷 Instagram.com/david_drazil

📘 Facebook.com/SketchLikeAnArchitect

💼 LinkedIn.com/in/daviddrazil

As featured in:

The Archiologist   gumroad   Archipreneur   teachable

Visuin   SCALE   VIZKON   morpholio

PH   SD   olgaart888   M

CPSIA information can be obtained
at www.ICGtesting.com
Printed in the USA
BVRC100832140921
616729BV00004B/22